A Journey from Slumber

A Journey from Slumber

A *Simple* Text for Life

By

Rachael Milam

ISBN: 978-0-6152-3563-9

www.ajourneyfromslumber.com

Printed in the U.S.A.

For Isaac and Emily

Upon the birth of each of you my heart, eyes and spirit were opened to the unlimited possibility of life's potential. I hope to be such an inspiration to you in your life's journey.

❊❊❊

Contents

❋❋❋

Foreword

R achael Milam is my dental hygienist. I met her three years ago when I retired and moved to the White Mountains of Arizona. She is one of those ladies always full of energy and always positive in her attitude. Even though she is already cute in a pixie way, her enthusiasm for people and life makes her much cuter.

Becoming a dental hygienist placed her in a healing profession. Now she has discovered that helping and healing other people in a new way is her purpose in life.

Her introduction to religion by her mother became a burden rather than a salvation. The overbearing and embarrassing nature of the denomination caused her to abandon it as soon as she left her mother's home. A transformation occurred as she passed through her years as a young adult. Rather than listening to another person teach her about God, she began to listen to that inner voice which we all have to some degree or another. As she became in tune with that voice and prayed to God, she received information and inspiration regarding the spiritual side of our lives. She came to believe that her greatest goal in life is to share this information with as many people as possible. The result is this book.

Rachael is neither a theologian nor a philosopher and she has received no formal traditional education in these fields that I am aware of. The obvious difference in her work is the short and simple delivery of her message. This format makes it easy and quick to understand. Hopefully, this aspect will encourage more working and family people, who don't have time to read novels, to pick this "simple text for life" and find a fascinating view of our spiritual lives.

— Gary Gatlin

❋ ❋ ❋

Acknowledgements

I must first acknowledge my friends, Gary Gatlin and Toni Roberts for the time and effort they put into editing my work. Without your keen eye and eloquent flow, I would still be struggling to make this book work. Thank you.

Thanks to all my friends and family members who have read, and then re-read and read my book again to give me feedback to make it better. I appreciate the time and effort you gave to help me on this project.

My final acknowledgement goes to my Heavenly Father for planting the seed of thought and for giving the means to allow it to come to fruition.

Introduction

Upon praying one Sunday morning, an idea came to me. I was giving thanks to God for allowing me to have so much in my life. I especially appreciate being able to rely on my INTERNAL COMPASS, which seems to keep me pointed in the right direction. At that moment of prayer, I received the inspiration that I needed. I had been praying for God to reveal to me how I may be able to make a difference in other people's lives. I believe this book was His answer. This story is about how I slowly and painfully learned to listen to the small voice within myself.

This is an account of my personal self discovery and how it unites with a basic understanding of the universe in which we live. I have discovered truths in this life that if understood and applied, will lead the way to a more joyful and complete life.

This book is a simple guide to assist others who wish to awaken their spirit within. As I share the lessons that have inspired me along the way, I hope that you too will feel inspired to improve the life that lies before you. No concept in this book is complicated or difficult. These suggestions are truly simple. Utilizing them only requires a desire for change, and a different perspective on life. And a little bit of faith both in yourself and in God.

Chapter One

⌘⌘⌘

My Beginning

The following is my story.

I was the second of four children born to a young couple who were trying to build a good life for their family. Religion seemed to be the focal point in my parent's life when I was young. My mother and father were baptized into a church that my father discovered around the time that I was born. Soon afterward my father decided that there were many teachings that he felt were too limiting on his life and just not right for him. My mother took the opposite viewpoint. She clung to her religion tightly and force fed it to her children. She took us, without our father, to church three times a week. We spent our Saturdays trying to convert others. I did not share her enthusiasm and felt embarrassed at having my school friends answer their front door, in their Saturday pajamas, so I could preach to them about our religious beliefs. Not until I became an adult did I appreciate the blessing of having been exposed to such a deep and sincere love for God.

After sixteen years of marriage, religion became a source of conflict for my parents. They had grown in opposite directions and no longer shared the same spiritual or personal paths. This separation ultimately led to their divorce. The difficulties of my parents became a defining experience in my life. Throughout that time, I was unaware that religious differences were the main cause of their disconnection. At the age of thirteen, I don't think that I could have experienced anything more painful than the dissolution of our family. As a result, I experienced distress so severe that it caused me to shut down emotionally. I went through the motions of my adolescent life on automatic pilot with my true feelings completely suppressed. Upon the dissolution of my parent's marriage the four of us children were divided between them.

In my first year of high school, during the first year after the divorce, I lived with my mother. I remember being introduced to behaviors that I had never previously been exposed to. My peers were bringing drugs to school and skipping class to get high. Fortunately, during this time I did not get involved with any of these things. I was still very innocent and inexperienced and was more fearful of the repercussion of my actions then interested in participating. However, I was depressed during that time and all I wanted to do was sleep. This was my way of escaping. I finally broke down under the continual unfounded accusations and criticisms by my mother. She irrationally micromanaged my life and made living with her unbearable, so I called my father for help. I moved in with him the summer before my sophomore year. I left my baby sister and brother behind with my mother. I was burdened by the feeling that I had abandoned them. Though, I did know that I could no longer live in such an ill-tempered environment. Living with my father meant more freedom and less parental supervision. His job required him to be away from home more than he was present.

With the combination of too much freedom, guilt and depression I made very poor choices.

I often experienced very powerful feelings that would overwhelm me. I believe the feelings stemmed from the guilt of poor decision making combined with the guilt of leaving my siblings behind, and depression. Because I did not understand what I was feeling, I coped by abusing alcohol. The alcohol numbed the feelings and kept me from dealing with the real issues. The more I drank the more poor choices I made. I look back now and see that during this time I was protected from irreparable consequences that could have greatly altered the direction of my life. The protection I felt was coming from my Heavenly Father. Even though I sometimes put myself in jeopardy, I was able to walk away without harming myself or others. It seemed that I was often struggling with something inside which I could not identify. I now understand that I was suppressing the positive intuitions from within. Deep in my being, I knew what it was that I *should* be doing, yet the conflict was with what I *was* doing. There was a sense of disharmony between my mind and heart. I knew it was up to me to learn how to escape the negative forces affecting my life, or continue down the destructive path I was on.

Finally, I had found a way through something my parents taught me. They had previously introduced me to meditation and other concepts that had the potential to lead me to self awareness. I could be quiet and still and soften the clutter in my mind. That allowed me the opportunity to be open to God's directives. Despite the fact that His messages were certainly strong, my ability to shut myself off from them was stronger. I wouldn't allow myself to listen. The messages I received confirmed the feelings I had deep down inside. I knew I was on the wrong path. Over time, I slowly allowed myself to open my heart to God's guidance. It took years for me to appreciate being exposed to positive concepts and really value the ability to be silent and listen to Him.

    After graduation, I left home as quickly as I could. I felt as though I was running toward something, not knowing what it was, but I was eager to get there. I was sure that things would be better once I was on my own. Little did I realize that no matter where I went, there I was. The same issues, feelings and pain followed me. The energy I was projecting out was that of a broken and needy person. I then met a man who I thought was "Mister Right." We fought and argued more than any couple I had ever known from the beginning of our relationship to the end. He was on a constant quest to find love and reassurance, as was I. I was definitely not the person who was capable of giving him all that he needed. I wasn't even capable of giving to myself what I needed. Twenty days after our wedding, he left for the Gulf War. He was gone for six months and we spent that entire time arguing over the telephone. Again, I experienced constant unfounded accusations and criticisms, this time from him. I felt myself reliving the very past I thought I had left behind.

    I began shutting down my emotions again, using my old coping skills from adolescence. It was too exhausting to maintain a loving connection with the constant negativity. What I did not understand was that by shutting myself off to the negative emotions, I also had shut myself off to all of the positive ones. Again, I escaped into emotional isolation. There were times when the world around me was dark, quiet, and free from distractions. I felt the pain deep in my heart. It was during these times, I began to hear God's message clearly stating that I was *not* where I should be. This message would literally make me feel sick to my stomach. I would rush back to bed to avoid the sensations with sleep. My greatest dilemma was being unsure of how to change my situation. Because I had made a decision to marry this man, I believed I needed to do everything in my power to make our relationship work. Over time, I realized the depth of my mistake and so I made the choice to leave my marriage. Soon after leaving, I knew that I had made the right decision because at nighttime, deep in my heart, I finally felt at peace. I knew within my soul that I was now headed in the right direction. I trusted that I would be led to where I needed to be.

That challenge of my life was a great learning experience for me. During that marriage, I experienced physical and emotional abuse that led me to discover my internal strength. I felt angry by his actions and that emotion empowered me to stand my ground. I learned to value myself even if the person who claimed to love me didn't. I learned to set boundaries and standards for myself. Never have I regretted marrying him, because our conflict eventually brought me to a greater understanding of myself and life. I do regret having to experience the abuse. There is never a time that it is okay to hurt anyone, whether you claim to love them or not. Without having realized it on a conscious level, my ex-husband and I were actually great teachers for each other. It seems that a person can learn the most about themselves during their most difficult experiences. I learned that I could not expect someone else to make me happy, nor was I responsible for someone else's happiness. I learned that it was impossible to try to help someone fill a void in their life that they are not even aware of. I found how to recognize when it was time to walk away while I still had the emotional resources to do so. Finally, I learned that when I followed the guidance within my heart, there was an abundance of strength that was available to help me move forward.

Chapter Two

Spiritual Guidance

We are never alone. There are loving forces that are constantly working to lead us to where we are meant to be. All we have to do is ask for help and trust that it will be there. The little coincidences we encounter daily and the larger miracles can all be attributed to a spiritual connection. We are all blessed with free agency, which means that we can choose to do whatever we wish without the interference of God. He allows us to do right or wrong, and He is willing to permit us to suffer the consequences of our choices, for our personal growth. But, if we desire His assistance, we must first request it. He will then be there to guide us and offer us comfort.

God has provided for us the heavenly direction we need while on earth. Jesus states in John 14:26, "But when the Father sends the Counselor as my representative, and by the Counselor I mean the Holy Spirit, he will teach you everything and remind you of everything I myself have told you." Our inner being is aware of this direction. We have this knowledge deep within us waiting to be tapped into and utilized. However, there is also temptation lurking close by, trying to divert us from our true path.

The feeling in the pit of your stomach, the surge of energy, the random thoughts that pass through your mind may not be there by coincidence. Be still and listen, the source may very well be a Spiritual Guide prompting you. You may be receiving direction from a higher source. Whatever entices us to do good is of God, and whatever turns us away from good is not of God. It is necessary to pray for confirmation of God's message when in doubt. We often know of His presence due to our feelings of inner peace. We must only recognize it. The following are experiences I went through while learning to listen to my inner voice.

I remember it clearly, as if it were yesterday. My new husband, six month old son and I were driving up a winding mountain road. We were discussing our future, and I threw out the idea of possibly going back to school to finish my degree. He encouraged me and promised to give me the support I needed. At that moment, I decided that this would be my new goal.

I worked part-time in the evening and stayed home during the day while my husband worked. We decided it would be the best for our family to alternate our schedules. That way we could also avoid the cost of childcare, which we could not afford at that time. I enrolled in evening classes the next semester at school as well as continuing to work at night.

Our family survived on a very small monthly income. We lived in a small home on an acre of land. Even though we did not have a lot of money, we tried to keep it maintained and as nice as possible. However, the home was starting to show signs of aging and it was beginning to deteriorate. On a rainy Sunday afternoon, I sat staring out of a window, watching the water dribble down. When I looked closer, I noticed a bit of mold growing in the window sill. I remember thinking, "*I cannot raise my son in a house that is falling apart and growing mold*." At that moment, I felt a surge of energy and knew that our lives had to change. Furthermore, I knew that I was the one who had to contribute more in order to make that change.

Our second hand computer gave me access to the classified ads on line. Immediately, I found an ad for a position that I wanted. The following Monday morning I called and was given an interview the same day. They hired me on the spot and I started my new job the very next week. Because of my feelings of restlessness and a surge of energy, I knew that I could make the change that we needed. By paying attention to the promptings that I was experiencing and by taking action to follow their direction, I was able to start the next chapter of my life. After some time passed, I really felt positive about our new circumstances even though we still lived in a house that was less than perfect. I knew that our living arrangements were only temporary and when the time was right, we would be able to improve them.

One inspiring afternoon, it seemed the right time to go house shopping. We had not formulated a plan other than wanting to be closer to the college I was attending so the commute would not be as time consuming. My husband was so trusting in me that he was willing to follow my intuitions alone. They had not led us astray up to this point.

Although we looked at several homes, none seemed exactly right. It was then that we found a housing development in an area that was ideal for my commute to school. The prices were manageable and they even offered us discounts on upgrades in the house. The contract dictated that we have it built beside homes that were much larger than ours would be. Since we did not really have any objections at that point, we signed the contract and gave them the deposit money that same day. As we drove home, we could hardly believe what we had just done. It was an amazing decision that just felt right. We were so grateful we went looking that weekend and just happened to stumble upon that particular home builder. It was completed and we moved in five months later.

On the morning of September 11, 2001, I was getting ready for work and watching the morning news, my usual routine. I was horrified to see the world as I knew it changed forever. As were most, I was shaken and moved by watching my fellow Americans suffer so needlessly. It caused me to reflect and evaluate the most important things in my life.

My sister and I were prompted to do something to show our support for America. We thought it would be fun to make lapel pins using little wooden hearts after painting them to look like an American Flag. It required hours of painting and gluing. We then gave the pins as gifts to family and friends. To my amazement, I received a request for 100 pins from an office in town. I got busy painting and gluing and sold the pins for a nice profit. More requests for pins followed the first. Those sales allowed me to start saving some significant money.

For some time, my husband and I had been trying to conceive another child. We had no success. Our son was four by then. We finally resorted to visiting a fertility doctor. That was an expense our insurance would not cover, and the financial strain limited our future attempts. I began debating over what to do with the extra money that I had made. It could be used to take a relaxing weekend getaway with my husband or we could see the fertility doctor one more time. I was encouraged by friends to see the doctor again, and felt that was the right decision. Even though our past attempts had taken a toll on our marriage, we still chose to go back to see the doctor one last time. If I did not get pregnant this time, I would no longer continue to put my husband or myself through more misery. If we did not succeed, it just wasn't meant to be. I realized that I could no longer control this situation. I placed it in God's hands.

On October 25th, 2001 our daughter was conceived. From the tragedy and death of 9/11, came an inspiration for me to show support for our country. From the inspiration to create American pins, to the decision to visit the fertility doctor one more time, I was guided throughout the entire process. That insight then resulted in the beginning of a new life. I was so grateful for this guidance, which I knew was not a coincidence.

I was now six months pregnant and prepared to apply for the dental hygiene program, for the second time. This college program chose their incoming students via a lottery system, not on academic standing. I wasn't lucky enough to be picked the first time around. Although I prayed that I would be taken on the second. My second rejection letter stated that I could be placed on an alternate list. Then should one of the original students decide that they did not want to enroll, I would be on the list to be given another opportunity. I considered throwing all their paper work away and not even submitting the reply. Who would drop out after spending all of the effort necessary to be selected in the first place? After I prayed, I felt that I had nothing to lose and if I did get accepted as an alternate, it would indicate divine intervention. A few weeks later, they called stating that I had secured a position in the class and could be starting the program in August. After quickly accepting, I considered all of the work that would be required and prayed that I had made the right decision.

What lay before me was one of the most frightening, but exhilarating chapters of my life. I would be starting a difficult, time consuming, course of study

and would have a new born baby to care for all at the
same time. However, the odds had been against me
when I became pregnant on our last attempt and the
odds had been against me when I was selected for this
school. Believing that God had provided both
opportunities, to be a mother again and a student at the
same time gave me the courage to attempt them
simultaneously. It was a comfort knowing that He would
not give me more than I could handle.

I made arrangements with family members to
come to my house and help with the children. When I
thought I had it all figured out, one week before school
started, my mother called me and said she wouldn't be
able to baby-sit on the mornings that I needed her.
Maintaining composure in the face of possible disaster, I
thought of another person whom I felt I could trust to
care for my baby. The big problem was that she lived 35
miles from my home and in the opposite direction from
my son's school. That meant that several mornings each
week I awoke my children and had them dressed and
ready to leave by 6:30 a.m. Then after traveling 35 miles
in one direction to drop off the baby with the sitter, I
traveled back in the opposite direction to get my son to
school before I ever started toward my first morning
class. It seemed as though my determination and
endurance were surely being tested. However, giving up
was never an option for me.

Occasionally we resorted to family pep talks for
encouragement. During these talks I once gave the
analogy that the four of us family members were like a
car with four wheels. Each one of us represented a tire.
If one tire was deflated, it caused the entire car to slow
down and made our journey that much more difficult for
everyone. As stress increased, there were times that my
husband and I were pushed to our limits. These times
were very difficult, but we are proud of what we were

able to accomplish together. It took the support of all of us, plus our extended family and friends, for me to reach my goal of graduating.

This was one of the most amazing ventures of my life. I received scholarships for academic achievements, and I managed to finish at the top of my class. I was honored with a special award for excellence in clinical skills that year. I know that I was blessed with all that I needed to triumph through that most difficult time. Through this entire process I felt as though I was being carried along by something greater than just my own efforts. I trusted from the beginning that if I did accept the challenge I would receive the help I needed, I was right.

After graduation, my husband and I took our children on a well deserved vacation. During our trip, I received a telephone call from one of the secretaries at the college. She told me that a dentist close to where we were vacationing had an opening for a new hygienist. I called and scheduled an interview. He hired me that same day. The doors were beginning to open right before us.

We had already put our house up for sale because we had planned on moving to this same area in the near future. We just did not anticipate that the future would come this fast. Now each step forward seemed to lead us to the next opportunity with ease. Our lives were now progressing faster than we had ever dreamed. We were so grateful for the guidance leading us in this direction. When we were faced with a decision the answer was contemplated and acted on. We knew we had made the right decisions when the doors began opening. If a decision was made and led us nowhere we then knew we had to reevaluate our situation and move in another direction.

We came home that next weekend and our house sold immediately. The value of our home had increased significantly due to being surrounded by the larger homes. We enjoyed a profit that we had never anticipated. We packed up our home in three days and moved into our rented house in our new community. We were eager to put down roots in our new home.

During the first year in our new home, I began to feel that familiar surge of energy. At first, it seemed to be that same restless feeling I would sometimes get in anticipation of a new discovery. However, this was different and I was unsure as to the source of this feeling. Usually I could tell when I was being prompted to move in a certain direction, and the direction was typically clear to me. I was confused as to what to do in this case. On one particular morning I felt inspired to share my uncertainty with a patient. I added that I was perplexed as to the meaning of this restlessness. His response was to ask me if I would be interested in buying a portion of his advertising business. His offer seemed a bit strange and was certainly not what I had in mind as to an answer. But, I told him I would consider it. I discussed it with my husband and we both agreed that this could possibly be a new opportunity for us. When the feeling of the insistent energy subsided, I knew I had found the answer which I was intended to discover. I trusted and followed through with my intuition. Intuition is God speaking directly to us. If we listen to Him we know what we need to do. As a result, my husband now owns a successful advertising business.

I firmly believe that each time I was faced with a choice to act or to be complacent, accepting the challenge lead me forward to the next segment of my life. Each stage of my life was built upon the last. There was not a moment of decision that I wasn't receiving divine assistance. Listen closely to the voice inside of you. It is trying to tell you something essential. Be open to the spiritual guidance and trust that God is communicating with you. All that you require will be provided, it is up to you to ask, accept, and act.

The following chapters present fundamental ideas and concepts that I found vital on this journey to live my life to its fullest. I learned how to ask for what was needed, accept and trust the answers that were given and how to move forward when prompted to.

Chapter Three

⌘⌘⌘

Gratitude

When I first shared the idea of writing a book with my son, he posed the question, "Is it going to be a text for life?" I asked him to repeat his question. He again said, "Is your book going to be a text for life?" After pondering his question for a moment I responded, "Yes, I guess it will be." In my opinion there cannot be any such text that covers the fundamentals of living a good life without discussing gratitude. Gratitude *is* the foundation for happiness.

It is easy to be full of gratitude when life is progressing favorably. Yet, when there are times of difficulty then it certainly becomes a test. That is when the true sense of gratitude is challenged. Gratitude is not just a word that is uttered occasionally. It is a deep and powerful feeling, a profound sense of peace and contentment.

Our lives may never be the ideal picture that we wish them to be. In reality they might turn out to be even better! Many people simply over look the gifts in their lives because they are always striving for bigger and better things. It is the recognition of the seemingly small "insignificant" blessings that give us a sense of fullness. Fullness in the sense that we now feel our life is filled with all that we need. It is vital to focus on what we do have and not what we are lacking.

We need to avoid the pitfall of looking at how other people's lives appear. This is a dangerous practice. We tend to spend too much time scrutinizing other people's prosperity, other people's belongings, or other people's social status. We often compare our lives with theirs. Although we can only see the superficial surface of their existence, we still try to imagine how we measure up. This is a very limited view of other people's reality. The outside picture is usually much different than what is actually on the inside. We often believe that everyone else around us has a better life than we do. It is at that point that we need to stop examining the outside appearance of others and focus on the inside of ourselves. That is where true peace in our lives begins.

Take a moment to reflect on what you do have and feel grateful for it. Look around you right now. What do you see? Are you inside a nice home, sitting in a comfortable chair reading this? Do you have eyes that recognize words and are you educated enough to read? Shouldn't you be thankful? You have a mind in which to formulate thoughts of gratitude and you have a heart to feel the fullness of the thought.

You can apply this concept to begin the process of meditation. With your eyes closed focus on this thought, repeating out loud or silently to yourself, "Thank you for giving me this life." Then spend a few minutes thinking about what you have said. Life is such a precious gift, such a wonderful opportunity for relationships, growth, and knowledge. There are those who cannot walk, see, smell, or even taste. These senses are examples of things we take for granted. Seldom do we recognize how lucky we are to possess these simple physical capabilities. Meditation should begin by contemplating the most simple and basic things we tend to overlook. Dwell upon them and appreciate them as gifts. Once you start to value these, your eyes and heart will become open to all of the other blessings around you. Blessings you may never have considered before. Reflect on how you would be if these gifts were lacking. Give thanks to God for allowing you to realize and treasure this gift of life.

With daily practice of giving thanks, gratitude will soon become part of your consciousness. Once acknowledging gratitude becomes a habit, you will find that your mind will automatically transition into a more positive response without it being a forced thought. This is a first step toward becoming a more thoughtful, grateful and loving individual. A wonderful feeling of happiness will grow within your being. Your mind will become open to the miraculous world of plenty that surrounds you. When we are lacking in the ability to comprehend what we have been given, our usual perception is that of discontent and want. There will always be desires for more in most people. They use "more" to try to fill the void that is seemingly always present. Not until we overcome the sense of dissatisfaction will we truly feel that we already have enough. Once we begin to truly have a sense of abundance, we find that more of what we desire subsequently arrives. By changing our mindset, we are also changing the energy within us. Whatever we dwell upon, our energy naturally draws to us. Is it rejoicing or a craving constantly in your thoughts? Whatever is on your mind will attract similar energy. This is covered in more detail in a future chapter.

When we are overjoyed what is our usual response? Whether we are feeling excited about experiencing something exceptional or receiving something special, our first impulse is to share with others. When we share the exhilaration with others, it is contagious. The excitement that is shared stimulates excitement in others. Inspiring others can re-inspire us and create a ripple effect. Reflect on this thought for a moment; *when I share good thoughts and feelings it creates more good thoughts and feelings.* Also consider the opposite; *when I am discontented and negative I bring about additional negativity in others.* Most of us wish to enjoy contentment and peace within ourselves, it begins with gratitude. We must recognize the little seemingly "insignificant" blessings around us that will put us on that road to contentment. Acknowledge that which is abundant around you and your world will improve. This I know to be true.

Begin your new outlook by writing in a journal. Note a few ideas each day that you are grateful for and review your notes often. Keep the attitude of gratitude and experience a transformation. See how much more positive your life becomes, and how people are drawn to you because of your good energy, and the optimism you have for life. It does take a conscious effort to accomplish this. Eventually, however, you will find that the pathways in your brain are altered and it is no longer a challenge to think positively. It becomes natural and normal for you.

I found that when I started to surround myself with uplifting people and spent time reading inspiring material, I found I wanted more. I couldn't read fast enough or show enough gratitude to keep up with the positive energy I was experiencing. It was natural to want to share these sensations with all of those around me. However, it was my experience as a child, that when someone believed something with an extreme passion, they frequently tried to force it upon others. Often it had the opposite effect. What I decided to do instead, was to live my life as an example. Therefore, I refused to talk negatively to others. I made it a habit to smile and share words of praise and encouragement with those around me. I tried to be the kind of person that others enjoyed being with. You can make it a point to uplift and inspire others by your positive nature and kind words. We all have days when we are not at our best. We are human after all. Just remember that you have a choice every moment as to the attitude you wish to express. Every day we can make a conscious effort to control our attitudes and communicate positively or negativity with others. It is our choice to make.

Know that it was not by chance that you are here on earth. Your life is not a fluke of nature. When you realize that there is a greater meaning to your existence, a sense of purpose will be created. When you have identified your personal purpose, thoughts of self worth are created. Again, it begins with gratitude. Writing and reviewing the notes in your journal will ground you with reminders of all that you have to be thankful for in this life.

It is important to understand *how* our thoughts affect our lives, so for that purpose, it is vital to review a few Universal Laws that I consider are necessary to create happiness.

Chapter Four

❄ ❄ ❄

Universal Laws

Law of Attraction

B y now, most of us have heard about the law of attraction and are familiar with that what we think about we bring about. It certainly may be one of the most talked about laws, yet it is *not* the solitary law of the universe. There are many universal laws that impact our lives. We adhere to these laws without knowing they exist. We break them without realizing the consequence. By obtaining a basic knowledge of these laws and understand how to use them to enhance our existence, we will find that we will live in greater harmony on this earth. The laws are intended to help maintain a sense of order on earth. Without these laws we would live in absolute chaos. Just as the social laws are placed in society to help us maintain order, the same applies to the universe.

There is a plaque that hangs in our home, it is a quote that we have all memorized, "*Thoughts become words, words become actions, actions become habits, habits become character, and character is everything.*"

The reality that everything begins with a thought is a powerful concept. What we think about utterly becomes our reality.

Our thoughts transmit a powerful energy. This is where that little seed of thought is nurtured and in turn is manifested into action. It is not possible to monitor each thought as it flows into and out of our mind, but with attentiveness we can distract our mind when we realize that we are entertaining negative thoughts. We can use a certain phrase or "mantra" that will put the mind right back on the path of positive or neutral thinking. Surround yourself with positive reminders of what you desire your life to be like. Make a collage of pictures showing you the end result of that which you desire or make a computer slide show, anything that is a constant reminder to your conscious mind. Allow the feelings of joy and excitement to fill you up when you see your future before you. Daily reminders will help draw to you what you are focusing on even more quickly. What you spend time thinking about will become fruitful. Be mindful of what you nurture mentally. Have faith that what you dwell upon will manifest. The universe will be working to bring all the pieces together. Have patience and continue to give it good thoughts. Don't ever give up on what you desire.

Law of Vibration

The next law that is important to discuss is the law of vibration. Everything in this universe is in constant motion. From the tiniest atom to the immense earth everything is constantly vibrating and moving. Energy is a force that can be measured and everything on earth has its own unique energetic rate or rate of vibration. Consider the motion of a top, spinning at a low rate its movement is noticeable, the faster it spins the more it appears to not be moving at all. The higher the rate of vibration the less the human eye can detect movement. As the frequency is lowered we can then again observe the top moving. In detecting sound, and seeing color the same principles apply. The higher the frequency the less likely we are to hear a sound or see certain colors. As the frequency is lowered the sound is again audible and color is again visible. Its presence is constant it may just be on a different frequency.

As human beings we each have our own unique frequency or rate at which our bodies vibrate and may be detectable by those around us. Some people are more sensitive to energy than others. Have you ever walked into a room where there was tension in the air? Can you remember sensing that feeling, without having knowledge of it before hand? If you were sensitive to the energy of others you would have sensed that there was a negative atmosphere present. The energy in this circumstance was in all probability thick and weighty and the frequency could have been measured as abnormally low. You were sensing the low vibrations being projected from an individual.

What about the opposite? Have you ever observed joy and excitement in someone that gives you chills? The energetic force they are projecting is so high it raises our energy just by observing what they are experiencing. We all project an energetic vibration with our thoughts and actions. Good or bad, we literally project the energy we contain out into the universe. We can either use this knowledge to our advantage by being conscious at all times or it can be used against us if we are not conscientious.

Gloom and negativity exist on a very low frequency. All the negative thoughts, feelings and actions reside in a place of low energy. Within a place of low vibration or energetic force is where mental and physical disease thrives. The opposite is true with optimism and positive thinking, actions and feelings. They reside in a place of high frequency, where the rate of vibration is soaring. Health is contained in a place of higher energy or vibration. It is difficult for the germ of disease to plant itself in a place the does not nurture it, or help it to flourish. Once disease has manifested itself in the body, it may be difficult to maintain a positive attitude or keep the momentum of energy high. We may not be able to end illness with just a simple positive thought, but we can certainly enjoy the moments of life a bit more with positive thoughts and feelings. Always remember that we are the ones that are in control of our thoughts and a simple thought is a seed waiting to be cultivated.

Again, what we project out comes back to us, whether we are conscious of it or not. If we are projecting low vibrations out to the universe, the universe ensures that is exactly what is reflected right back to us, in equal amount. What a comfort to know that we can consciously propel out those loving and creative thoughts and we will be rewarded. This is one way we can be assured that our metaphorical cup will maintain fullness. The knowledge that we are the ones who choose is something we should consider with mindfulness and not to be taken lightly. Here again it is reinforced that we do create our own reality by what we think.

We need to be selective of whom we spend our time with. There are those who will deplete our energy and bring our rate of vibration down to their energy level. Do not stay around people like this for very long. Do not become overly involved in their experiences. Love them from a distance if possible. Live your life from a place of higher energy and allow them to learn from you and from your example without them depleting your energy. Instead, spend your time with those who are on the same energetic level as you are or higher. It just feels better to be around these people, you somehow walk away feeling energized.

Law of Rhythm and Cause and Effect

Imagine for a moment the pendulum in a clock, swaying from one side to the other. There is a certain rhythm created to maintain balance, the further it swings to the left the further it will come back and swing to the right. Such as the rhythm of life, day turns in to night and night into day; a baby is born and an old person passes on. There is a certain rhythm to life that is seemingly inescapable. How about our feelings and moods? They are subject to the law of rhythm as well. We all experience feelings of elation, yet at some point it may be followed by feelings of depression. What goes up must come down, right? It is the law of Rhythm after all. What if with a greater understanding of ourselves and this principle we were able to rise above or escape the effects of this law when it comes to our feelings and moods? Is it absolutely necessary for our moods to ebb and flow to such a degree? The swing of the pendulum seems to swing on an unconscious level, back and forth it goes without any thought given. With greater awareness we do have the ability to rise above this law without suffering the effects of the inevitable swing. Just as if we were sitting above the pendulum watching it swing, we are able to avoid the negative counter swing by being aware of it. This does not mean that we avoid the extreme feelings of happiness, for fear having to experience the opposite. On the contrary, the more joy we feel and experience the more joy we will feel and experience. This concept is not an easy one to master, but with desire and consciousness it is possible. Our Will is the solution if we truly desire the balance we can achieve it.

"Every Cause has its Effect; every Effect has its Cause; Chance is a name for a Law not recognized." The law of cause and effect is simply "What goes around comes around", or Karma. We may not know why things may happen, good or bad, but they all happen as a result of either a known or unknown cause. There is no such thing as chance. Thoughts we think, actions we take, either consciously or unconsciously, have an end result. There is no way to avoid the impact of this law.

What if, instead of being a pawn in the game of life, you were the one making the moves on the great chess board? Think for a moment of the ideas you have and the desires you hold in your heart. Where did they come from? Were they someone else's ideas or desires first? Were you influenced by someone you perceive to be stronger or wiser than yourself? It is sometimes easier to place claim on other peoples conceived ideas, than it is for us to take the time to delve deep into our own mind to discover our own true desires and ideas. What if, you could be the cause in charge of the effect? With awareness of your thoughts and actions you can be.

While we cannot always control the world around us, what we can control is our thoughts and our behavior. We can make conscious choices that bring us closer to living in harmony with God and the universe. The closer we stay in tune with these forces, the more peace, guidance and direction we will enjoy.

By moving toward mastering our mindfulness, living with faith in ourselves and in God, by listening to our bodies and keeping our minds healthy, we will be on the path that will lead us to the state of inner peace, balance, and contentment.

There are many more laws that keep our universe in check, but for simplicity's sake I have reviewed a few that I feel are critical to understanding and mastering the balance of life.

Chapter Five

✖ ✖ ✖

Perception and Action

Perception is defined as, "The process of acquiring, interpreting, selecting, and organizing sensory information." The word perception comes from the Latin *percepio,* meaning, "Receiving or collecting." It is important to understand the definition of perception since the meaning is the only part of perception that is the same for everyone.

The view we have of the world around us, the feelings that we experience and the life we create are all manifested by our individual perceptions. I remember hearing as young child that I created my own reality. This was a concept that was very difficult for me to comprehend. How could *I* create the world around me? How could *I* control the environment and people the around me? At the root of creating my own reality was my perception of the world. If I saw the world as a horrible place and felt negative about my existence, which I often did, that was exactly what I experienced. That became my reality.

I now know that my life is much more enjoyable when I live with a positive outlook. When my perception is that of goodness around me, this is then reinforced by

the experiences I encounter. The more I focus on that
reality, the truer it becomes for me. It is also true that
the world around us can be unpredictable and
frightening at times, we cannot control that. However,
we can make the best of what comes our way by being
conscious each moment of the choices that lie before us.
By being aware of how we *act* and not just automatically
responding to life around us, we then have the ability to
manage our perception, therefore creating our reality.
Each person has to decide whether to see the "glass" half
full or half empty. This can determine, to a great extent,
how happy our lives become.

It is up to each one of us to raise or lower our
energetic frequencies to create a positive or negative
sensation. We do this most often out of old habits.
Depending on the perception we have of each significant
event we experience, we organize the placement of that
energy into a positive or negative compartment. We are
then raising or lowering our frequency to match our
perception. I found that for myself, while growing up, I
had a tendency to most often place my experiences into a
negative compartment. It seemed to require less effort
and to be more natural for me. It was my automatic
default. It was easier to think the worst and react with a
pessimistic impulse as opposed to consciously raising my
energy by moving into a positive mode. I felt normal in
responding that way. The experiences I had, justified
why I responded the way I did. After all, I was just
reacting to the world around me. It was a knee-jerk
response done without conscious reflection. To *act,*
rather than react, when you are in a certain situation is
to reply with an intentional purpose. You are then
invested and take greater responsibility for the end
result. Consequently, you can actually decide what to do
during any situation. By consciously choosing to raise
your frequency, you can create positive energy. You then

become the one in control of the aura around you simply by being mindful and aware of your thoughts.

Perception is a process of acquiring or taking in information, interpreting or analyzing that information, then deciding how to respond to that information. For example, another driver cuts you off in traffic. You immediately process this experience and interpret it by thinking this guy must be an inconsiderate jerk. You feel angry and frustrated by his actions. You put out to the universe negative energy and thoughts about this person in this circumstance. As a result, you allow this person to take away your happiness for that moment and replace it with anger. You were then thinking only of yourself and how you were affected by his behavior. Did you stop to consider that maybe there was an emergency or another good reason why this person did what he did? When we allow our automatic assumptions to be ruled by negative thoughts and feelings, it is amazing that we seem to continue to encounter the same situations over and over again. We are drawing to us those experiences by our negative response. Although we cannot change how other people behave, we can change ourselves. We can learn to let it go, by letting the moment pass without giving it any significance. If we truly understand the consequences of negativity we would be a bit more careful of avoiding it. What we think about, we bring about.

The next time that you encounter a frustrating occurrence, take a deep breath and silently put out to the universe that you bid that person well and they must have had a good reason for their actions. Whether you believe they did or not, stop yourself from automatically generating negative energy. Do not allow another person to take away your contentment, even if it is for only a minute. Allow this moment to pass without wasting your thoughts and energy on something that is meaningless.

Think for a moment about an annoying person you recently met that relates to the philosophy above. Were you driving in traffic or shopping at a store? How did you react? Did you respond with anger? Now give a second thought to this experience. This time change the outcome in your mind to a positive one. See yourself being unaffected by the trivial matter. Imagine you smiling at the person and bidding them well. By practicing attentive responding, you can program your mind to think in a certain way when encountering a certain situation. When you are purposefully planning a positive response, you are creating your reality. It will be a more positive reality. It all begins with the seed of one thought.

Perception is not a passive thought process, it produces action. We are consistently gathering information about the world around us and interacting with it through our actions. When someone is suffering from depression, they can feel somewhat paralyzed. It may be difficult for them to even get out of bed. Their negative perception of the world is creating a negative reality therefore the result can be an inability to cope. This is an example of how extreme negativity can produce physical consequences.

Perception and action go hand in hand. If you are suffering from a pessimistic outlook, and are not sure how to begin to change it, start with your actions. Do something positive. Help an elderly person load their groceries into their car. Open a door for someone. Even a simple smile to a stranger is a powerful action. Doing something kind for someone without expecting something in return can bring change to your life. Act with love and kindness as your intent. Your energy will begin flowing in a positive manner. As you begin to feel the positive energy, your thoughts will follow in kind. Thoughts will follow actions and actions will follow thoughts. So, both think and act consciously in a positive manner. This may feel uncomfortable when you begin, however that is the start of change. Be consistent in your actions and soon it will feel natural. You are reprogramming your mind beginning with little acts of kindness, becomes positive thinking. Actions will generate energetic momentum.

Controlling our actions seems to be one of the most challenging things for us to master. If we are to create change in our lives, some form of action is required. Positive action results from determination plus motivation. Often times the lack of motivation that keeps us from moving forward is a lack of clear direction and goals. We may feel overwhelmed by too many choices. This can cloud our options and make us afraid of making the wrong choice. We often find it easier to stay within our *comfort zone*, where we know what we are capable of, with a somewhat predictable outcome. This keeps us from having to work hard at a new directive that might be incorrect. The less we attempt, the less opportunity there is for failure. Yet, there is also less opportunity for learning and expanding to obtain higher success. Too often our responses are both automatic and unintentional. When we become introspective, we may just discover what we truly desire in our life. Spend time reading material and investigating that which may peak your interest. Go to a book store and walk around. See what subjects you are drawn to. You may discover an interest you never considered before. Write in a daily journal. This may help uncover ideas that you may not be aware of that are contained in your mind.

Rome wasn't built in one day and neither was the creation of our ideal lives. What do you want your life to be like? Decide what qualities you admire in others that you would like to possess. Search the inside of yourself and identify those things that you would like to change or add to your character. Once your inner person is reflected upon start looking at your environment and your immediate surroundings, what would you like to do to make it even better? After you identify your desires, you can then start to create a plan. Begin like you were making an outline for a story of your life. You should find that once you begin to log ideas on paper, the pieces will begin to put themselves together, creating a visible path you may wish to follow. Once you know where you wish to go, the less anxiety you will have and the clearer your mind will be. This clarity allows you to gain momentum. That momentum will turn into action. It first begins with the seed of a thought.

Remember that it takes an initial surge of energy to get the momentum going toward change. Pay attention to the voice inside of you which tells you to proceed in a given direction. Then do something to head that way even if it is small and seems insignificant. Make that first move. It is absolutely vital to get you to the next phase. Smile at strangers. Help someone else. Take care of yourself. The opportunity for positive action is waiting for you.

Keep your eyes wide open and your heart receptive to the possibilities that await you. I believe that sometimes we spend too much time contemplating and not enough time acting. We can think ourselves right out of the action we should take. It was strange to think that I would impulsively go house hunting and so quickly find a home that suited us. The result of that action, taken from the little voice inside of me, turned out to be wonderful for my entire family. Don't miss opportunities by being complacent, fearful or reluctant to act.

I have found that when I venture out of my comfort zone and challenge myself with the unknown, I am lead to places I had never imagined existed. Once on that journey, I find that the necessary energy is there waiting for me to tap into. Similar to giving birth, it is hard to believe that you will have enough love and energy to give to his new life. But once the baby arrives, they bring with them all the extra love and vigor that is needed for the parent child journey together. It is the same with giving life to a new idea or venture. All that you need you will find comes to you upon the birth of a new idea.

Energy, Action and Love are all abundant on this earth. The more energy you put out, the more energy you find you have. The more often you act, the easier it will become to take that next step forward. The more love you share, the more love comes to you. You must stop thinking your way out of opportunities and start listening to your instincts that project the momentum for a great life.

I am not implying that you act impulsively and put yourself in any unsafe position. I am not suggesting that you jump into something that has not been given any thought and did not **feel** like the right action to take. Our feelings and our instinct are an important guide in helping us to know if the decision to take action is the right one. If it doesn't **feel** right, then don't do it. However, if it does seem right do not continue to question until you talk yourself out of taking action. Take the action that feels correct when it seems to be appropriate or you may be missing an important opportunity.

I can't stress enough how important positive actions are in life's equation. We are constantly flooded with new thoughts and ideas. Spend time praying and meditating upon those ideas that won't leave you alone. These promptings may come from deep within you. When you ignore them and do not respond, you miss opportunities for growth. Life requires that you take action. Get up and move. Enjoy this world around you that was meant for your exploration and inspiration. You will find what you need if you do not procrastinate.

There are so many paths in life that lie before us. By being conscious as to the guidance that is within you and with consistent prayer, the best path will be made clear. You will have confirmation that you are where you need to be by observing the doors that will open before you. They will seem to say, "Welcome, we have been waiting for you." Then start in this new direction knowing that you are where you need to be at this time. However, if it seems doors are being closed in front of you, maybe it is time to stop, pray and listen. The answer will become clear in your mind and heart. Do not ever allow yourself to become complacent and fail to go forward because of indecision. You cannot care for or serve yourself or anyone else if you cannot move. Do not ever allow yourself to become complacent by indecision. Inaction will leave you in a stagnant place as long as you allow it to. Then time will pass as your opportunity for knowledge and personal growth is wasted. Instead, seize the opportunity now. It is never too late to start. If you are just waking up from a long period of inactive slumber, take a deep breath, find your resolve and prepare yourself for a rewarding journey.

Chapter Six

Prayer and Meditation

Prayer is a way of sending to God, all that lies within our mind and heart. We may be asking for guidance and help with life's difficulties, or we may be giving thanks for all that we have. There is a constant link between us and God that requires only that we ask Him for what we need. Once we ask it is then up to us to listen for the answer.

We are meant to be here. We made a covenant with God and agreed to experience life on earth. We have a specific mission to fulfill. Each one of our missions is different. It is not necessary to fully understand what our mission is ahead of time in order to be successful. However, we all have a common responsibility which will help us to reach our goal; that is to love and serve each other. That was Christ's mission. He showed unconditional love to each human on Earth, even up to the time of his death. He served man everyday of his life because he loved us and he wanted to be an example for us. He was the perfect example. If we remember his life's mission it will give us what we need in order to accomplish our life's mission. Those two simple things are Love and Service.

When we were born a veil was placed over our minds. This veil keeps us from consciously recalling our memories of being with God, but the possibility of thinning the veil is within all of us. This life on earth is a spiritual schooling and offers us a great opportunity for our personal growth and the chance to assist those around us grow as well.

This human life is a test. If we remembered everything from our spiritual past, this would not be much of a test. Each moment we are being tested, we have a decision to make. Do we act out a negative impulse? Do we pause and consider consciously the implications of our actions and instead choose to act with love and kindness? The decision we make will greatly affect our future growth.

I found, in my spiritual development, that I got to the point that I was constantly, silently praying. Not just asking for help but giving thanks for the opportunities that I was experiencing. When I was challenged, I began to recognize that it was a chance to help me to grow. It was up to me what choices I made. If I was resentful and angry with the situation, I had just failed that test. However, if I elected to pause and reflect on what I needed to learn, I had passed the test. If I wanted to do better than just pass, I needed to formulate a positive response. Yes, even when I wanted to run in the other direction. I began looking at every situation that frustrated me in a different way. I then understood that I needed to seize every opportunity, both good and bad, for growth and enlightenment.

Now, I literally give thanks for challenges, even those that frustrate me, for growth that I might not otherwise have had. I have been known to literally thank the person and their reactions have often been ones of disbelief, which in turn lightened the atmosphere and turned it into a pleasant encounter.

This may sound a bit unrealistic for some, but when you remove your ego from the equation and really contemplate your purpose in life, your ego becomes insignificant. We can recognize it as a limitation or road block to reaching our potential. It became more important for me to find humor and joy then to be right or have the last word. What a fun challenge.

Recognizing that our perception of ourselves is a huge factor in the way that the world views us is vital to understanding the ego. I began by using meditation to discover who I really was. Not how the world viewed me on the outside, but who I truly was on the inside. What uniquely made me, Me. Meditation is the opportunity to listen to God and to the universal forces. Prayer is asking. Meditation is listening.

Meditation allows your mind to be quiet, calm and relaxed. Let the difficulties and questions you are struggling with flow out from your heart and mind. Do not hold on to them. Concentrate only on breathing. It is that simple. Breathe. Spend as much time as you need until you feel a calmness come over you and your body feels relaxed. During your time of meditation you can either think of nothing, but just your breathing or you can practice focusing on one specific thought.

I have a specific CD that I listen to while I rest. It is a color balancing CD with positive affirmations. It is not necessary for you to be awake during this time, as your mind will absorb and process the words while you sleep. Using color balancing in conjunction with positive affirmations, works to put your body in balance and your mind at ease. I found that when I was really out of balance I would do a combination of meditation and visualization for three consecutive nights. A noticeable feeling of peace and clarity would result. I rely upon this technique of mind and bodywork to help me to stay clear, centered and balanced.

This is how I balance my spiritual mind and body. There are many different methods available to try. Once you find one that works for you, it will truly make a remarkable difference in how you feel. Be creative and see what you can do with your visualization and affirmations. Make it unique to you and have fun.

Chapter Seven

✖✖✖

Affirmations and Visualization

Affirmations are positive expressions that you speak to yourself. They can be contemplated silently or they can be said out loud. They are words repeated over and over to condition your mind to accept what you are trying to reinforce.

If you find yourself in a special situation, such as a competitive event you can use this affirmation technique to give you an edge. Repeat over and over again in your mind or out loud the outcome you desire. Focus on it. Continually affirm it and visualize it and soon it will become your reality.

During my college days I visualized how my graduation or special ceremony for my class would proceed. I wanted to give a speech expressing to my fellow peers and my family how very much I appreciated them for all that they did to help me achieve my goal. I envisioned details of how I felt standing there speaking. How my family swelled with pride at my accomplishment. I put a lot of emotion into how I wanted the day to go. Now, I did not share this vision with anyone. I just would go over the speech I wanted to give in my mind, and visualize myself standing in front of my peers and family. As the time approached, my class began planning for this special day. They were organizing the event and deciding who would be giving speeches. I happened to be nominated by them to represent our class. You can imagine the excitement and gratitude I felt that I was chosen. I just put out there what it was that I desired to achieve and kept the vision in my mind. I left the rest up to the universe and it didn't let me down. Did the day happen just as I visualized? Yes it did, with all the emotion and pride that I had envisioned.

Visualization is another very powerful technique. It is a tool which can be used to train your mind. You must name what you want before you can claim it. Visualization is the vehicle that enables us to identify what we desire. We must first conceive a thought in our mind then add specifics to the thought. The thought may be, "I want to be truly happy." You must next search your heart to find the things that bring you happiness. Picture them in your mind. See yourself smiling and truly enjoying getting those warm fuzzy feelings during your visualization. These pictures will manifest themselves into your reality over time. The more emotion you feel when you visualize, the faster it will manifest. Our brain is a human computer. What we put into it is the reality of what we become.

Our subconscious mind is the obedient and willing servant to our conscious mind. It does not discriminate, nor does it analyze good or bad. It just does what our consciousness tells it to. When we continually focus our conscious mind on a certain thought or vision, our subconscious wants to close the gap between reality and what we are thinking of. So, the energy is then focused and released. The result is the creation of circumstances that will help bring what it is we have been focusing on. Be careful of the thoughts you entertain. You are creating without even realizing it. Again, the situations we desire will manifest themselves. It is our responsibility to recognize and control our thoughts and act upon them to make them a reality.

Through our five senses we continually perceive the world around us. We are formulating thoughts and feelings about what we are experiencing. By allowing our ego or outer self to make vital decisions, it may often times lead us in the wrong direction. We need to use our conscious mind and listen to the promptings deep within to find the answers. We need not care or give consideration as to how others may perceive our decision. They are probably contemplating how you are viewing their decisions. It is wasted time. Spend the energy meditating and visualizing the life you want to create for yourself. Focus on that!

The opportunities that await us are limitless when we use visualization as a tool. It is comparable to loading information into a computer. You put in to it only what you want to use. Be careful of saturating your mind with negativity. Television, movies and violent images also become programmed in our mind. These things draw upon the energy resource that we have and deplete us. Instead, consider spending your time more wisely by choosing to download files that will be a source of strength you can call upon when needed.

It has been proven, scientifically, that our brain cannot differentiate between running a race in our mind and actually physically experiencing the race. We go through the same process mentally during both. This became a profound and powerful realization for me. I thought, "You mean I can just visualize what it is that I would like my life to be and the process will begin?" That is absolutely correct. You must first conceive of the idea. Life is full of potential. Dream big and visualize big. We often limit ourselves due to lack of faith in ourselves and feelings of being inadequate. We are the ones that place the restrictions on ourselves. Even if you grew up in a family where you were criticized and felt unworthy of living a great life, you too can begin to change your life by visualizing something different and great for yourself. What do you have to lose?

Remember you are not alone. All you have to do is *ask* for help, and it will come to you. Even if you do not know what you desire, *ask* for the answers to be given to you. It is then up to you to *listen* for the answer. Have faith. This life was meant for our growth and spiritual development and enjoyment. Have fun with your creation. Always remember, "Thoughts become words, words become actions, actions become habits and habits become character....and character is everything."

This was a powerful realization for me. It helped me to really understand the force behind our mental and emotional energy. I did not allow one negative thought to enter my mind. I thought only of what I wanted and not of the fears that I had of speaking in public. We are always going to feel emotions when preparing to experience the unknown. They can be uncomfortable and somewhat overwhelming. It does not, however, need to be debilitating or limiting. Keep your thoughts on what you desire and of the final result you wish to come about. Try it, you just may be surprised.

Chapter Eight

✖ ✖ ✖

Attitude and Intent

The attitude we carry gives life to the energy around us, that energy is continuous. We are the ones that propel the vibration of positive or negative. Our attitude is what creates what we feel inside and what we send out to the world.

When we embrace a perspective of being grateful and recognizing the gifts that are all around us, more of that good energy is drawn our way. We act as a magnet to energy either positive or negative.

Have you known people that just seem to have "bad" things keep happening to them? Wherever they go they seem to attract trouble? Life is a continual struggle for them and nothing seems to go their way? It may very well be due to the attitude they carry, as well as the intent of their heart. We may be able to fool the world around us, but the universe and the life force that surrounds us cannot be fooled. Energy is, in fact, a measurable real thing and we need to recognize its existence so we are not unconsciously using its power.

On the other hand can you think of people that seem to have it all? They just keep attracting to them more of the good stuff. Even if they do encounter trouble in their lives, they seem to be able to turn it into a positive. Life seems to just flow and things always seem to work out. It usually isn't by chance. They have figured out that they are 100 percent responsible for the actions they take and the thoughts they think. They also recognize the power that lies within.

The world around us can be frightening and unpredictable, as some may perceive it, or it is a magnificent place full of opportunity. Our perspective is the determining factor. It is not that we deny the things that may go on in this world, but recognize that we can help to change it. Everyone can make it a better place by carrying with them an attitude that accepts full responsibility for the experiences that create their lives.

At every moment of everyday we are faced with decisions, choices and opportunities. With each decision, each choice and each opportunity we are sculpting our life. We are the masters of our own destiny. Therefore, we must choose wisely. Our decisions need to be made consciously. We must be willing to see the possibilities that lie before us with an open heart and without fear. Fear is often blinding. We may not see the opportunities due to its influence. Fear is nothing more than a symbolic noose that keeps us stuck, stuck in the memories of the past and the illusions of the future. We fail to appreciate and grasp the opportunities that are here in the present moment. The next time you are faced with a decision, big or small, give conscious thought to the power you hold within. Ask yourself, "Am I making or not making this choice due to fear?" You may be surprised by the answer. The decisions we make may be life changing or something seemingly trivial. Do not underestimate your response to either.

A seemingly, *simple* choice you may be faced with, is whether or not to participate in gossip. This simple decision may seem somewhat insignificant, yet it may be a life altering moment. Not only do you feel better about yourself for not contributing to the negativity that is being slung all around, you are also setting an example for those that are gossiping. They may not notice it at the moment, but the next time they are back biting hopefully they won't try to include you. Then the next time that you are inevitably faced with this situation you will feel more empowered. Each time it becomes easier to consciously choose. Do not be afraid to be different. Embrace the positive good energy and more of it will come to you. You will realize that moment, if you had given power to the negative thoughts and participated in the gossiping, how you would have created more negativity. It always comes full circle. While others are stuck in a negative place, by making a thoughtful decision to exercise self control, you are free to move on.

Life on earth is just like school. No one jumps from kindergarten straight to college. Hopefully, we learn as we experience life, so that eventually we will be prepared for advanced enlightenment in the future. Everyone can move forward as long as we have paid attention and seized the opportunities to learn at each step of the way. It is necessary to accept that the situations we encounter, negative as well as positive are placed there as a chance for growth. Everyone has the power to make a conscious choice regarding each matter they face, big or small.

The first and most important thing is to accept full responsibility for your life. Are things fantastic? Great, then you are on the right track. Keep living mindfully and have fun with your life. However, is your life a little less than what you had hoped for? Are you constantly faced with challenges that seem overwhelming? Believe it or not you are the one with the power to change that. You are not being punished by God, without life's many challenges growth is not possible. He is not making you suffer intentionally there must be something you need to learn. He has provided all that you need here on earth in order to create the life you dream of. Life is full of abundance and opportunity. You will be faced with many more decisions. Make your choices cautiously with deliberate consideration. That doesn't just mean careful actions, but careful thoughts as well. Remember, the attitude that you carry is the only thing you can really control.

Intention is the underlying force behind attitude. You may say one thing, yet feel or act in a different way. Do not underestimate the power of intent. It is the root to your motivation and the force of creation. If you spend time meditating and reflecting on your life's intent you will find the answers. It is as though you are looking at your life under a microscope really understanding yourself at a deeper level. You may discover elements you didn't even know existed within yourself.

Intent will ultimately push its way through to the surface, manifesting itself in your attitudes and actions. If you continue to go about life without being attentive, you will be continually acting and thinking without awareness. The consequences may be making the same mistakes over and over again and getting the same results repeatedly. In turn, if you slow down and take the time to be introspective as to the meaning of your intent, you will attain personal awareness. This will be the start of truly discovering who you really are. You can then explore what it is you were placed here to accomplish, and what your life's mission may be. It will at least put you on the path to discovering this truth. This discovery may not be as hard as it may seem. It requires only desire for change and faith, faith in you and faith in God.

Consider for a moment the idea that you were a spirit long before taking on physical form and coming to this earth. You were a co-creator with God. You helped originate this opportunity for spiritual growth through this earthly experience. All you have ever known and all that you will learn on earth is not lost with the creation or loss of a physical body. All of your wisdom acquired throughout your past remains with you. You may not be able to consciously tap into it as you may tap into a childhood memory, but it is there. You are a Being with an incredible ability to create. Unfortunately, many people limit themselves with debilitating thoughts. These limitations may have started when you were a small child, "You can't do that." The limits placed on you by respected authority figures are too numerous to name. They were placed on you by their fear for you or their own personal fears. FEAR is the key word. What would have happened if you were allowed to explore without being told that you couldn't do it? Knowing that the watchful eye of someone loving was there to help you if you needed it?

God is the loving source of help that is always there for you willing at any time to offer assistance. He only requires that you ask. He will not interfere in your life of free will, unless you request it. You are allowed to create on your own, without limits placed on you. There are no limits, only fear of the unknown.

Imagine that you have unlimited ability to create the life that you thought you could only dream of. You have the ability to be the Michael Angelo of your blank canvas. Spend some time going deep inside yourself and identify what it is you would like to start painting. Do not limit yourself by questioning how it will manifest, it will come. It is the universe who will create the situations that will allow your dream to come true. It is then up to you to recognize the opportunities and act on them. Do not be fearful, you will have lost nothing by acting. On the other hand, if you do not act you will have lost an opportunity that may have allowed you to pursue your dream. Also, you may have lost the confidence in yourself necessary for the next challenge.

Start out each day being mindful and faithful. Let the fear you may have dissipate. Fear is only an *illusion,* but it can be incredibly debilitating. Negative thoughts are like a self imposed weight around our neck. They bind us to the limits we place on ourselves due to fear. Imagine if each one of us lived to our potential, the amount of love and positive creation would overwhelm the earth. What a wonderful place to be. This is what God had envisioned for you. This is what you had planned with him for yourself before you were born on this earth. You create these imaginary barriers that keep you from being all that you were meant to be. Lift the barrier and move forward, all the help you need is waiting for you. All you have to do is just ask.

Chapter Nine

❊ ❊ ❊

Self-Confidence & Ego

Most of us determine who we are through our ego. The definition of ego is, "Self." Our ego is often used as a measuring devise. It is how we view our self and is the image we project to others. It is understandable in the world we live in, the apparent importance of the ego. If you show weakness or insecurity you are viewed and judged accordingly. We may feel a need to inflate our ego in order to equip ourselves with what we think is necessary for success on this earth. We try to keep people from seeing our true nature and the ego is a shield that facilitates that. We may not even be aware of who we are on a deeper level due to the immense influences of the ego. We may be driven by an idealistic view of what we see as important to appear as assured.

Once you begin to recognize and identify who you are internally, you will find that things around you become much clearer. Your motives will be less and less driven by the ego or how you are perceived by the outside world. There will be a new force driving your decisions and actions. This link to the inner self is more closely connected to God, where there are less distractions and confusion. There is confidence abound when we strive to live more from our inner self than from the ego or manufactured external self. Our true intention and desires become clear and the choices we make will put us on the path to peace and contentment.

Upon learning to trust and listen to your intuitions, you will begin to build confidence in your abilities, and recognize that your decisions will lead you in the right direction. Believe in yourself. Know that you have a perfect internal guidance system inside of you waiting for you to access it. Believe that you are divinely guided and protected and all that you need can be shown to you upon your request. You are a worthy, lovable human being full of so much potential.

Self-confidence is not the same as being driven by the ego, there is a stark difference. When your ego is in charge you are not listening to your inner self. You are focusing on outward appearances, and how to make things *appear* to look good to the outside, as opposed to truly feeling good on the inside. If you are balanced and centered on the inside, the outside will naturally reflect that.

Self-confidence is just that, trusting and having assurance in yourself; knowing that the inner self will lead you in the right direction and that you can rely on the reason for the inner self leading you there. Over time that trust will come and you will place greater and greater confidence in your abilities. Be patient and allow yourself to grow at your own pace.

When we are allowed the freedom to be challenged we slowly build confidence in our abilities. When we are challenged and excel at something this helps in creating self-confidence. When expectations are kept realistic for the age and perfection is not expected, children will naturally glow with pride at their accomplishments. It is important to allow children the freedom of exploring their own abilities and learning the lessons that come with both success and failure.

If that opportunity was not given, or you were constantly criticized for not performing to certain standards, you may need to return to the beginning. This may involve some reprogramming. Be gentle with yourself, see yourself as that small child and consider how it makes that child feel when you have negative perceptions. Be conscious of how you see yourself and what you say to yourself. Allow yourself the opportunity to become what you didn't have the chance to as a child, a confident and secure being. Start out with simple tasks that you will certainly excel at. When you do perform well, acknowledge it and allow yourself to feel good about it. Avoid the negative self talk that tells you that it was not good enough. It is your turn to decide what is good enough now. There was only one perfect person that ever walked the face of the earth and it wasn't you or I. Keep your perspective realistic and don't forget to make it fun. This life was meant to be enjoyed. We take things way too seriously. We often suck the fun right out of life when we look at it as a burden. Then we spend our time only existing not living life to its full potential. There is so much joy and happiness just waiting for us to embrace it.

Often time people use drugs, alcohol or other means of escapism to deal or *not* deal with the daily experience of life. Escapism could be extreme television watching, excessive computer use or video games and sleeping. When we use escapism we are missing out on some great lessons life has to teach us. Spend some time considering if you use a form of escapism to cope with life. If you do, ask yourself why, what are you trying to avoid? If you cannot figure this out on your own, *ask* for help. Seek out a professional who can help you discover why you feel the way you do, and help teach you to overcome these feelings you have about yourself and your life. With some help you will be able to move forward and see that life is certainly manageable and can be a joyful, wonderful experience. You may not have been given the tools necessary as a child to construct the life you desire, but you can still acquire them. Choose to start building today, no matter what your age.

Just as when we were children, we find that we sometimes need help. Often we are still that little person who has grown into a big body. It is important to remember that it is okay to *ask* for help when we do not know. Spend time in prayer *asking* for direction and guidance. Go to the library. *Ask* for the book you need to jump off of the shelf at you. *Ask* for whatever it is that you may need. We were given free agency when we came to this earth and that means that we have the privilege to build the life *we* choose without interference from God or any of His spiritual beings, UNLESS we *ask* for help.

Chapter Ten

✕✕✕

Self-Responsibility & Self-Reliance

We often take the credit for life when things go our way, but the moment life goes awry it is easily seen as someone else's fault. It seems much simpler to place the blame elsewhere than it is to accept responsibility for an unwanted outcome. It is the great Ego that may be making an appearance at moments like these. We don't want to *appear* weak or fallible in the eyes of others. How can we possibly learn from our mistakes, so as to avoid making them again, if we don't even take credit for them in the first place?

Take a moment to reflect on the accomplishments in your life. Think of the decisions and choices you made that have placed you where you are today. Each choice that has been made has an end result attached to it. Do you recognize that you are ultimately the one that made the choices which landed you where you are today? You are the one that can take credit for your great decision making.

There is not a person out there that does not continually error. It is in our nature to make mistakes.

The true question is, do we learn from them or do we keep making the same mistakes over and over again? Until we accept 100 percent responsibility for our shortcomings, we will continue to go over the same lessons again and again. The beautiful thing about being human is each time we error *and* we learn from it we are advancing in this earthly school. This is all part of our growth as individuals. Humility and self-responsibility are two remarkable qualities of an aware person.

Taking responsibility for our lives is not just centered on making good or bad decisions and accepting the end result. It is about learning about us, and having a vision for our lives, then following through with the actions necessary for achieving success. Take the initiative to educate yourself. It is vital to have sufficient knowledge, in order to have the information necessary to make responsible choices. I am not referring only to having an advanced education, although it seems mandatory in the world we live in today. I am simply referring to gaining a vast knowledge base of many different topics. The better equipped we are with an expanded awareness the more wise and intelligent decisions can be made.

The concept of self-responsibility includes the way we care for our bodies inside and out. By making wise choices as to what we put into our bodies from food to drugs or alcohol, we are doing what we can to be responsible for maintaining good health. Engaging in good habits will help to keep our bodies functioning at their optimal level. Moderation is the key to finding balance in all things. When we find that we are continually overindulging we need to take the time to be introspective as to what it is we are trying to avoid. The longer we overindulge and dodge the issue, the further detached we become as to the cause of the unbalance. We start to create unwise habits that compound the issues at hand. It is much wiser to tackle the problems that we encounter as they come up. If we feel the desire to escape this is our cue to dive inward and search for the answer.

Truly inspiring people are the ones that accept responsibility for their decisions and the results of the decisions, good or bad. They do not dwell upon the appearance of how their decisions seem to others. They make decisions to the best of their ability and accept responsibility for the outcome, humbly. They recognize that life is much more fulfilling when they look at what lies before them with a sense of gratitude and excitement. Each adventure is seen as an opportunity to learn and grow beyond what they thought was possible. There should be a deep sense of reverence as to the blessing of this life on earth. To take any possible opportunity for growth and knowledge and not use it to its full potential is to be given a gift and then throw it away. Accept this gift of life, be grateful for it, and take responsibility for its budding potential. Become one who inspires others and lives life to its fullest.

Self-Reliance

The words that often echo inside my mind are words of advice from my own father, "You must be able to support yourself. There is no guarantee that someone will be there to take care of you." Spouses die, situations change, life is forever throwing something new at us. It is our responsibility as men and women to be able to adapt to life's ever changing situations. This advice was not meant to imply avoiding relationships, but instead, to seek out relationships with people that share a like-minded vision of themselves and their lives.

If you are a self-reliant individual and you venture into a relationship with a person that is dependent upon you to fill all of their needs, you may find yourself drained in a short amount of time. Relationships like these sap the very life out of you. In time you may see the effects of its poison, either physically or mentally or both. When we seek out individuals who are in the process of "becoming" self-reliant or are already to that point, there lies a great amount of potential in a relationship. When two people are bogged down by the excess baggage of emotional, mental or financial issues, they spend their energy just trying to maintain the status quo. Imagine the potential that lays with a couple that each have individually worked out these issues and now are ready to move onward and upward together in this adventure of life. They will be so much further advanced, each contributing vital knowledge and energy to ensure success. By being mindful as to *who* you choose as a partner and *why* you chose them, you will either add a degree of difficulty to your life or you will progress beyond your wildest dreams.

There are so many aspects to self-reliance; financial, physical and emotional, each equally important. When we become dependent upon a source other than God and ourselves, we may be forced to make decisions based upon desperation, not clear purposeful intent. We may find ourselves at the mercy of others to fulfill our basic needs. This leaves us open to potential deception. When I was 18 and married *Mr. Right,* I made that decision based upon fear of not being able to care for myself. Once I was fully immersed in that situation I found how dangerous and delusional it really was. It was at that point my dad's message chimed again. I worked hard to get a job that could sustain me on my own. When I was ready, I found the courage to escape, without looking back. From that point forward, I vowed to never allow myself to be in a situation based upon desperation. There are too many options available to us, and too many loving people out there that could be of support in helping us find the right path. Never should we settle or compromise our values or standards out of fear. There is a better way.

Chapter Eleven

✖ ✖ ✖

Love

Love is a striking word. In our language this is the best verbal expression of something we have a great affinity for. Have you ever felt so much love that this word didn't seem like enough to express how deeply you felt? Love, being such a powerful declaration or expression, is something we all desire to feel and desire to share. It is an amazing sentiment, with unlimited potential for creation.

Love is the reason we are here. Learning to love and to be loved is the ultimate test. Loving without conditions, not just each other, but ourselves as well is the quest we are all on and are something we all strive for. We have the perfect example set before us, the example of Jesus Christ. His message was clear, but to consistently apply what it was he taught seems a bit more difficult.

Self love appears to be the most difficult and challenging lesson to master. We often times are overly critical and unrealistic in our expectations of ourselves. Are you able to look at yourself without being overly critical of your imperfections? When you look at yourself do you only see your shortcomings? Can you see yourself as a wonderful, kind person that is capable of being loved and loving others? Do you have a preoccupation with yourself or do you only think of others and what their needs may be? If we are thinking only of other people and not ourselves, we are neglecting ourselves. Just as thinking only of ourselves keeps us from successfully serving others, there is a fine balance to achieve between self and others. It requires that we are in tune with our inner self. We must make sure that our cup is filled to a level that allows us to share, or we may find that we have nothing to offer in the means of loving service.

Imagine for a moment, the next time you are thinking a negative thought about yourself, that you just spoke those words to someone you care deeply for. Imagine the hurt you would have just caused, and the depth of the pain you just inflicted. You are no different. Be conscious of what you speak and think quietly to yourself. Regard yourself as a valuable and important person, someone that you would never intentionally consider inflicting pain on. Someone you truly love. Loving ourselves first is the foundation for truly being able to love others.

The less critical you are of yourself, the less critical you will find yourself being of others. You will find that you are more accepting of those things in which you cannot control. The more you focus on maintaining your proper thinking the more you will allow others the freedom to be who they are. Often times we try to control things outside of ourselves because we are feeling like we cannot control the things within.

How do we get the love from another person that we need? It first starts with *giving* the love to them. Stop dwelling upon the frustration you feel with not *getting* what you desire and start *giving* what you desire. Once you start giving what it is you want to receive, you will find you start getting just what you need. Remember the Golden rule? "Treat others the way you want to be treated." This is certainly true in giving and receiving love. You are showing the other person exactly the way you need to be loved. Often time's words cannot express what we need. Actions are more easily understood and easily imitated. So, the next time you feel frustrated for not getting what you need, stop and rethink your method. Give to the other person what it is you desire and see what happens.

I have experienced this very circumstance. I spent years in frustration at not getting what I needed in my marriage. I found that I was slowly deepening a wedge between my husband and myself with the anger and frustration I felt. I remember finally thinking the thoughts mentioned above. I thought, "What do I have to lose?" I had to remove my powerful ego from the equation. I was able to give without resentment. My ego was responsible for deepening the wedge between us. I allowed myself to give to him what I needed with love, kindness and sincerity. I *slowly* started noticing a softening in him, and a gentle kindness returning. He felt and acted more loving toward me, and in turn began *slowly* giving to me what I needed. I reinforce the word *slowly*, because after years of behaving in a certain way, it takes time to gain trust and amend the damage that had been done. Be sincere in your words and actions. In time you will begin to find that you both will be receiving what you need. Love, it is the beginning and the end of all that we strive for. There is a perfect balance that needs to be achieved, and it first begins with loving ourselves, just as God loves us.

❀❀❀

One Final Thought

T he personal accounts I shared in this book were meant to reveal that there is nothing unique about me or the situations that I found myself in. I experienced discontent and recognized an imbalance with where I was in my life. I acknowledged the need for change. That alone was the catalyst that created the momentum for altering my life. I learned the fundamentals one painful lesson at a time. As I stumbled upon what I felt was a *key*, I placed it in my heart for safe keeping and went on. When I came to the place in my life when I actually felt content and balanced, with a sense of complete fullness, I fell to my knees in tearful prayer. I was completely overwhelmed with gratitude and joy. I knew that somehow I needed to share the information I gained. That is when the Lord planted the seed of thought for the creation of this book. I humbly accepted the challenge. This book reveals the *keys* I discovered on my personal journey. I encourage you to take this information and put it to the test. You will be amazed by your results.

There are times in all of our lives when we are brought to our knees by struggle, lack and limitations. It is my hope for you that you too, will come to the point when you fall to your knees in tearful prayer at the utter gratitude and joy you feel for your life. At that point, you will know all that is necessary to live the life you were meant to experience.

May your journey be rewarded with the sweetness of inner peace and joy!

❈ ❈ ❈

Bibliography

McCune, Dr. S and Milanovich, Dr. N. The Light Shall Set You Free. Albuquerque, NM: Athena Publishing, 1996.

Three Initiates. The Kybalion, Hermetic Philosophy. Chicago, Ill: Yogi Publication Society, 1912, 1940.

Webster's New World College Dictionary, Third edition. New York, NY: Simon & Shuster, Inc. 1997.

www.ingramcontent.com/pod-product-compliance
Lightning Source LLC
LaVergne TN
LVHW011411080426
835511LV00005B/487